MW01001025

ARIZONA CACTI: AN INTRODUCTION

There are more than sixty species of cacti found in Arizona, and this field guide will enable you to identify the most common desert species. Those which are rare or difficult to identify have been omitted, making it quicker and easier to learn the more common species.

This guide is one in a series designed to acquaint the layman, student or tourist with the common plants and animals of Arizona–many of which are curiously adapted for life in a harsh environment.

There is real pleasure to be had from gaining a fundamental, practical knowledge of your surroundings; and what begins as a casual interest may develop into a hobby or, in some cases, a career.

Whatever your interest, keep in mind that it is against the law to collect cacti without a permit. Enjoy them, but please do not dig them up or otherwise injure them.

HOW TO USE THIS EASY FIELD GUIDE

When you have singled out a cactus for identification, look at the plant carefully. Then start at box 1 on the next page and see which of the two different characteristics apply to your specimen. Then continue to the page indicated by your choice, and continue from there until you have narrowed your choices down to a particular species of cactus.

The black area on the range maps indicate the usual habitat for each specimen listed in the guide. For orientation, the upper dot on the range maps represents Phoenix; the lower dot represents Tucson.

Cacti vary greatly, depending on age and location, so do not expect the living plant to look exactly like our drawings. A hand magnifier may be useful for determining certain characteristics. There is a checklist in the back of the guide where you may record your observations, and a sample glossary defines the seven terms we refer to in the text.

IDENTIFICATION OF CACTUS GROUPS

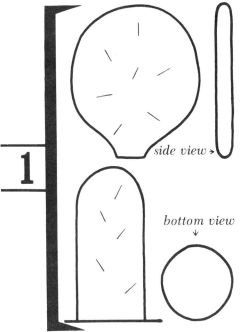

side view →

bottom view ↓

1

If the cactus you are looking at has stems that are flattened, turn to page 14 and see exactly what kind of
PRICKLY PEAR CACTUS
you have.

If the cactus you are looking at has cylindrical stems, turn to page 2.

IDENTIFICATION OF CACTUS GROUPS

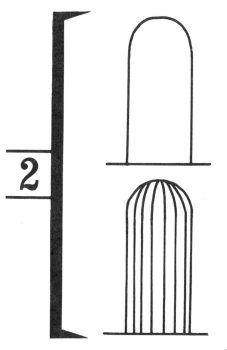

If the stem does not have continuous ribs that run from top to bottom, turn to page 3.

If the stem does have continuous ribs that run from top to bottom, turn to page 4.

IDENTIFICATION OF CACTUS GROUPS

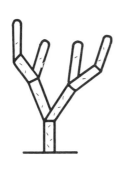

If the cactus has branches, turn to page 6 and see exactly what kind of
CHOLLA CACTUS
you have.

If the cactus does not have any branches, turn to page 18 and see exactly what kind of
PINCUSHION CACTUS
you have.

3

IDENTIFICATION OF CACTUS GROUPS

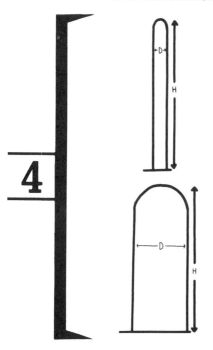

4

If the height of the stem is at least 10 times its diameter, turn to page 20 and see exactly what kind of
CEREUS CACTUS
you have.

If the height of the stem is less than 7 times its diameter, turn to page 5.

IDENTIFICATION OF CACTUS GROUPS

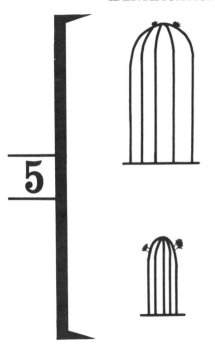

If the diameter of the stem is 5 inches or more and the fruits and flowers grow from the top of the stem, turn to page 22 and see exactly what kind of **BARREL CACTUS** you have.

If the diameter of the stem is 4 inches or less and the fruits and flowers grow from the sides of the stem, turn to page 24 and see exactly what kind of **HEDGEHOG CACTUS** you have.

CHOLLA CACTI

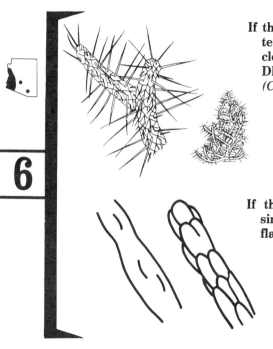

If the stem is covered with flat-tened, diamond-shaped tuber-cles, it is a
DIAMOND CHOLLA
(Cylindropuntia ramosissima).

If the stem is smooth or has simple tubercles which are not flattened, turn to page 7.

CHOLLA CACTI

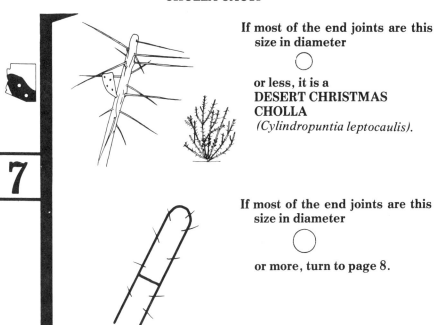

If most of the end joints are this size in diameter

◯

or less, it is a
**DESERT CHRISTMAS
CHOLLA**
(Cylindropuntia leptocaulis).

If most of the end joints are this size in diameter

◯

or more, turn to page 8.

CHOLLA CACTI

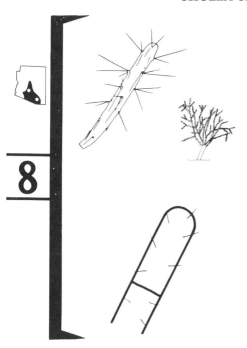

If the diameters of most of the end joints are this size

**or less, it is a
PENCIL CHOLLA**
(Cylindropuntia arbuscula).

If the diameters of most of the end joints are this size

or more, turn to page 9.

CHOLLA CACTI

If the fruits are dry and have long spines, turn to page 10. (There may not be fruits on the cactus you are trying to identify. In this case, it will be necessary to find a similar specimen that does have fruits.)

If the fruits are fleshy and have no long spines or only a few, turn to page 11. (There may not be fruits on the cactus you are trying to identify. In this case, it will be necessary to look for a similar specimen that does have fruits.)

CHOLLA CACTI

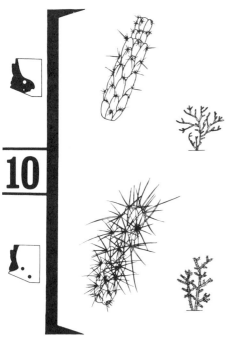

If the stems are reddish green or bluish green and the tubercles are 2 to 3 times as long as they are wide, it is a
BUCKHORN CHOLLA
(Cylindropuntia acanthocarpa).

If the stems are gold or silver colored (including the spines) and there are many long spines and the tubercles are less than 2 times as long as they are wide, it is a
SILVER CHOLLA
(Cylindropuntia echinocarpa).

CHOLLA CACTI

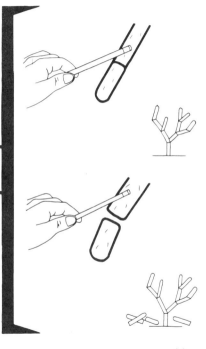

If the joints cannot be easily knocked off by rapping them sharply with a pencil, or if there are very few joints on the ground, or if the fruits remain on the plant all year, turn to page 12.

If the joints can be easily knocked off by rapping them sharply with a pencil, or if there are many joints on the ground, or if the fruits do not remain on the plant all year, turn to page 13.

CHOLLA CACTI

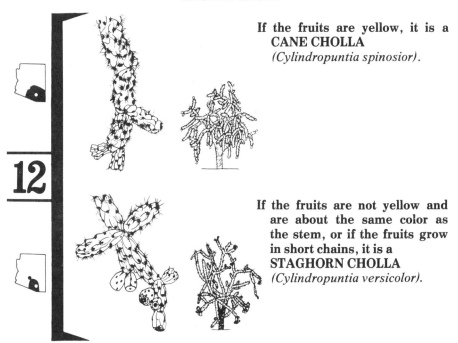

If the fruits are yellow, it is a **CANE CHOLLA** *(Cylindropuntia spinosior)*.

If the fruits are not yellow and are about the same color as the stem, or if the fruits grow in short chains, it is a **STAGHORN CHOLLA** *(Cylindropuntia versicolor)*.

CHOLLA CACTI

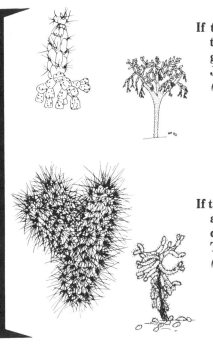

If the fruits grow in chains and the joints resemble the diagram on the left, it is a **JUMPING CHOLLA** *(Cylindropuntia fulgida).*

If the fruits do not grow in chains and the joints resemble the diagram on the left, it is a **TEDDY BEAR CHOLLA** *(Cylindropuntia bigelovii).*

PRICKLY PEAR CACTI

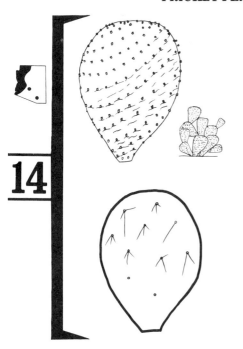

If the stems have no long spines and the cactus is found within the range shown on the map, it is a
**BEAVERTAIL
PRICKLY PEAR**
(Opuntia basilaris).

14

If the stems have at least some long spines, turn to page 15. (There are a few spineless varieties of prickly pear other than the Beavertail. They occur in the eastern part of Arizona and are not included in this guide.)

PRICKLY PEAR CACTI

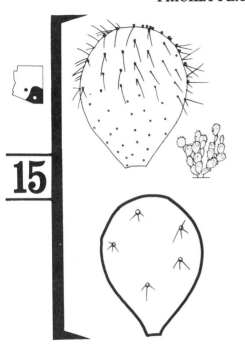

If the stems are purplish, it is a
PURPLE PRICKLY PEAR
(Opuntia violacea).

If the stems are not purplish,
turn to page 16.

turn to page 16.

15

PRICKLY PEAR CACTI

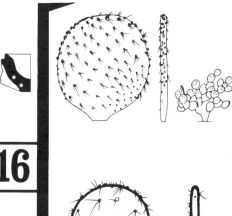

If all of the long spines (with the possible exception of those on the edges) point downward next to the stems and most of the stems are round, it is a **FLAPJACK PRICKLY PEAR** *(Opuntia chlorotica)*.

16

If some of the long spines (other than those on the edges) point outward or upward from the stem, turn to page 17.

16

PRICKLY PEAR CACTI

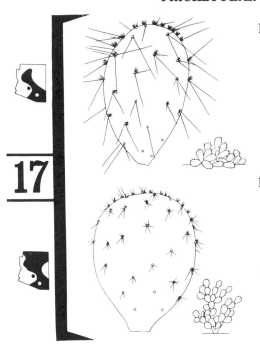

If the plant has a tendency to grow close to the ground and has few stems--if any--that are as long as 6 inches, and if the long spines are much more abundant on the upper halves of the stems, it is a **SPRAWLING PRICKLY PEAR** *(Opuntia phaeacantha)*.

If the plant does not have a tendency to grow close to the ground, and if many of the stems are at least 6 inches long, and if the spines are about equally distributed between the upper and lower halves of the stems, it is an **ENGELMANN'S PRICKLY PEAR** *(Opuntia engelmanni)*.

17

PINCUSHIONS

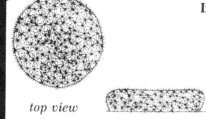

top view

side view

If the top of the cactus is flattened or depressed, and if none of the spines are shaped like fishhooks, it is a
CREAM PINCUSHION
(Mammillaria gummifera).

If the top of the cactus is not flattened or depressed, and if some of the spines are shaped like fishhooks, turn to page 19.

18

PINCUSHIONS

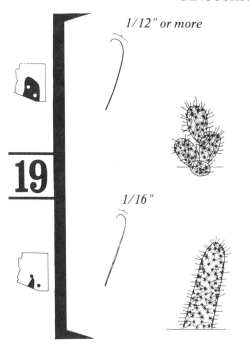

1/12" or more

If the hooks on the ends of the central spines are this distance across

⊢—⊣

or larger, it is a
FISHHOOK PINCUSHION
(Mammillaria microcarpa).

1/16"

If the hooks on the ends of the central spines are this distance across,

⊢—⊣

it is a
THORNBER'S PINCUSHION
(Mammillaria thornberi).

19

CEREUS CACTI

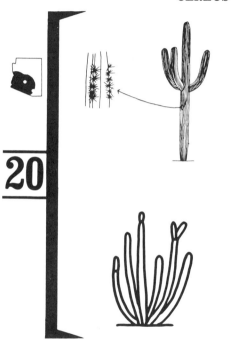

If the cactus has only one main trunk at ground level, it is a **SAGUARO** *(Carnegia giganteus).*

If the cactus has a number of stems at ground level, turn to page 21.

CEREUS CACTI

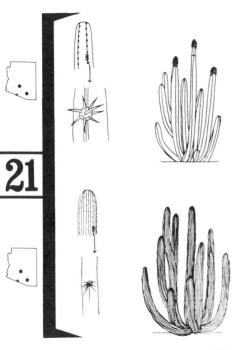

If the stems have 9 ribs or less, it is a SENITA *(Lophocereus schottii).*

If the stems have 10 ribs or more, it is an ORGAN PIPE CACTUS *(Lemaireocereus thurberi).*

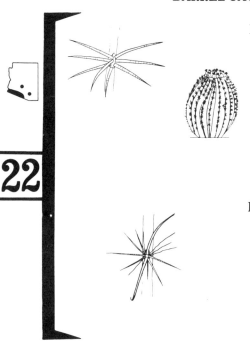

If all of the radial spines are very stout and are not flexible, it is a
COVILLE'S BARREL CACTUS
(Ferocactus covillei).

If at least some of the radial spines are slender and flexible, turn to page 23.

BARREL CACTI

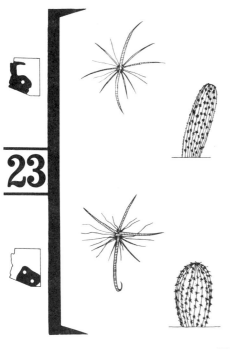

If the main central spine is not
hooked like a fishhook, it is a
**COMPASS
BARREL CACTUS**
(Ferocactus acanthodes).

If the main central spine is
hooked like a fishhook, it is a
**FISHHOOK
BARREL CACTUS**
(Ferocactus wislizeni). .

HEDGEHOG CACTI

If the areoles are elongated and the stems have bands of different colors, it is an
ARIZONA RAINBOW CACTUS
(Echinocereus pectinatus).

If the areoles are nearly round and the stems do not have bands of different colors, turn to page 25.

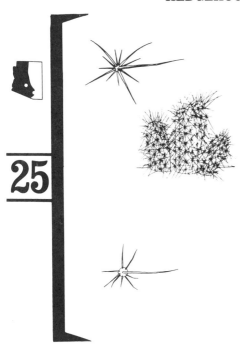

If the main central spine is somewhat flattened or twisted and the other four central spines are well developed (giving the stem the appearance of being very spiny), it is an
ENGELMANN'S HEDGEHOG
(Echinocereus engelmanni).

If the main central spine is round at the base and is not twisted, and if the other spines are not very long, turn to page 26.

HEDGEHOG CACTI

If there is one central spine and the number of radial spines on each areole is 11 or less, it is a **FENDLER'S HEDGEHOG** *(Echinocereus fendleri).*

If there are 2 or more central spines and 12 or 13 radial spines on each areole, it is a **FASCICULATUS HEDGEHOG** *(Echinocereus fasciculatus).*

CHECKLIST: COMMON ARIZONA DESERT CACTI

	Locality Observed	Date
CHOLLAS		
DIAMOND		
BUCKHORN		
SILVER		
DESERT CHRISTMAS		
PENCIL		
STAGHORN		
CANE		
JUMPING		
TEDDY BEAR		
PRICKLY PEARS		
BEAVERTAIL		
PURPLE		
SPRAWLING		
ENGELMANN'S		

CHECKLIST: COMMON ARIZONA DESERT CACTI

	Locality Observed	Date
PINCUSHIONS		
CREAM		
FISHHOOK		
THORNBER'S		
CEREUS		
SAGUARO		
SENITA		
ORGAN PIPE		
BARRELS		
COVILLE'S		
COMPASS		
FISHHOOK		
HEDGEHOGS		
ARIZONA RAINBOW		
ENGELMANN'S		
FENDLER'S		
FASCICULATUS		

GLOSSARY

The following terms are used in this guide:

AREOLES — Little structures on stems of cacti from which spines grow.

CACTI — Any plants which have areoles.

CENTRAL SPINES — Spines (usually longer than the radial spines) located in the centers of the areoles.

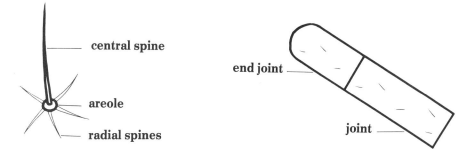

GLOSSARY

JOINT — One distinct section of a cactus; an "end joint" is the last joint.

RADIAL SPINES — Spines which are located around the edge of an areole.

STEM — In this guide, the terms "stem" and "joint" are used interchangeably.

TUBERCLES — Bumps on stems.

The following plants are often mistaken for cacti, but they are NOT; they do not have areoles.

OCOTILLO

YUCCAS

AGAVES